CAMPING
in the BUSH

Contents

CAMPING IN THE BUSH

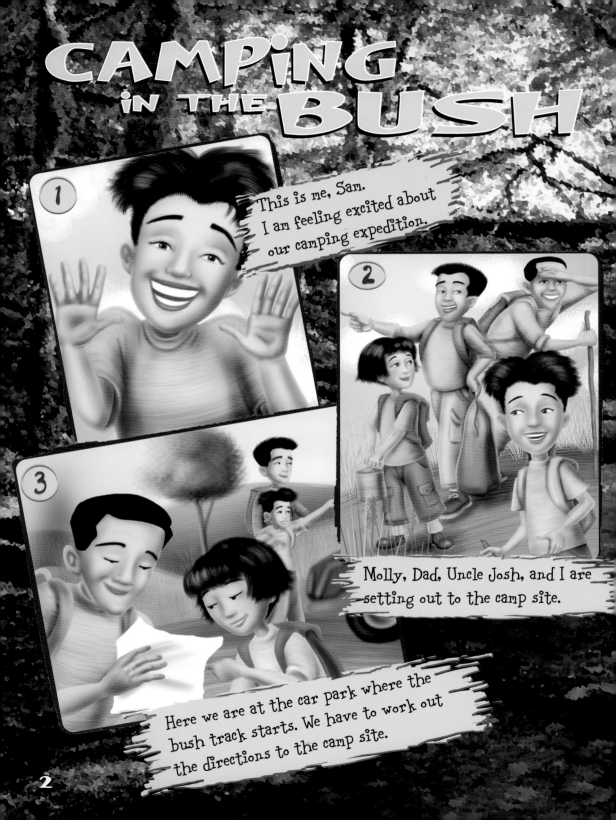

1 This is me, Sam. I am feeling excited about our camping expedition.

2 Molly, Dad, Uncle Josh, and I are setting out to the camp site.

3 Here we are at the car park where the bush track starts. We have to work out the directions to the camp site.

DIRECTIONS TO CAMP SITE

1 Walk along the path until you reach the rocks at C1. Climb over the rocks.

2 Continue along the path until you reach the bushes at A1. Turn right and keep walking.

3 You will see a bridge at A4. Go over the bridge and keep walking.

4 Follow the path through the forest at C5.

5 Turn right at the abandoned cabin at D7 and keep walking.

6 Follow the path around until you get to the stone arch at G6. This is where the path ends.

7 Go through the stone arch and walk in a westerly direction for about five minutes. You will see the camp site up ahead.

Erecting a TENT

1

Here we are, erecting our tent at the camp site.

2

Dad is reading the instructions and looking perplexed.

3

Oops! Back to Step One!

HOW TO ERECT A TENT

You Will Need:

a tent

a centre pole

four tent pegs

a hammer

STEP ONE

Spread the base of the tent out flat on a cleared piece of ground with the rest of the tent on top of it.

STEP TWO

Lift the top of the tent with the pole, then place the end of the pole in the centre of the tent base.

STEP THREE

Hammer the tent pegs through the loops at each corner of the base.

STEP FOUR

Put the pointy end of the pole in the middle of the top of the tent.

CLARIFY!

perplexed

A worried

B happy

C confused

A, B or C?

Making a SHELTER

Dad thinks we should give up on the tent. We will make a shelter instead.

INFERENCE

What inference can be made about Dad?

HOW TO MAKE A SHELTER

Materials you will need:

seven straight branches

string to tie the branches together

lots of leafy branches

STEP ONE

Find seven branches as tall as you are.

STEP TWO

Choose the strongest of the branches you have found and set it aside.

STEP THREE

Stand three of the branches up so that they form a tepee shape.

STEP FOUR

Tie these branches together at the top. Now, the tepee should be able to stand on its own.

STEP FIVE

Repeat Steps Three to Four with the remaining branches.

STEP SIX

Tie the strongest branch across the V made at the top of each tepee shape.

STEP SEVEN

Stand the leafy branches along the frame in overlapping layers.

Making a BUSH BED

1 We forgot the mattresses. The ground is very uncomfortable. Molly is complaining.

2

Dad has a brainwave. He is examining the fern.

3

Fern is really comfortable! Dad is pleased with himself.

HOW TO MAKE A BUSH BED

Materials for a Bush Bed

bracken fern

a sleeping bag

- Collect lots of ferns.

- Place a thick bed of cut ferns on the base of the tent.

- Throw your sleeping bag on top.

- Try it out!

Synonym = A word or phrase that has a similar meaning to another word or phrase

Find the synonym for

base

A   a part on which something rests or provides support for

B   a compartment

C   the lining

A, B or C?

Making a SOLAR STILL

1

Problem! We have discovered Uncle Josh has left the water bottle in the car.

2

I am adamant I will not drink water from puddles.

3

Uncle Josh has a brilliant idea. He suggests making a solar still to purify water.

HOW TO MAKE A SOLAR STILL

Materials for the Solar Still

something to dig
a hollow with

one cup

two plastic bags

five rocks

muddy water

PREDICT●●●

How do you think these materials will be used to make a solar still?

PROCEDURE FOR MAKING A SOLAR STILL

STEP ONE

Dig a shallow hollow in a sunny spot.

STEP TWO

Line the hole with one of the plastic bags.

STEP THREE

Put the water from the puddle in the hollow.

STEP FOUR

Place a cup in the centre of the hole.

STEP FIVE

Put the other plastic bag over the hole, letting it sag a little in the middle.

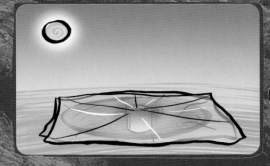

STEP SIX

Place four rocks around the outer edge of the plastic bag to keep it in place.

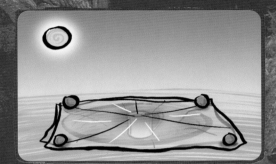

STEP SEVEN

Place the last rock on the plastic bag directly above the cup so that the plastic slopes down in the centre.

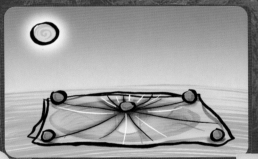

QUESTION?

What devices are used to help make the instructions clear?

CLARIFY!

sag

A to sink
B to hang
C to fall

A, B or C?

Making a SOLAR BARBECUE

1 We are starving! Molly has found some sausages and we are ready to cook them.

2 Dad is trying to explain he didn't bring any matches. He is concerned about how to cook the sausages.

3 Uncle Josh has another brilliant idea. He suggests a solar barbecue.

HOW TO MAKE A
SOLAR BARBECUE

You will need:

one box (for example
a tissue box)

some foil

scissors

a piece of wire

one cereal packet
for cardboard

QUESTION?

Why do you think foil
would be needed in a
solar barbecue?

PROCEDURE FOR MAKING A SOLAR BARBECUE

STEP ONE

First, take the tissues out of the box and cut the box in half.

STEP TWO

Now, use one side of the cereal box to make a curved surface.

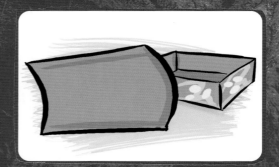

STEP THREE

Cover the curved surface with foil and place it in one half of the box.

QUESTION?

Why do you think the side of the cereal packet needs to be curved?

STEP FOUR

Place the half box lined with foil inside the other half box on a slant.

STEP FIVE

Put one sausage on the wire, and push it through from one side of the box to the other so that the sausage is near the foiled surface.

STEP SIX

Finally, place the whole barbecue in bright sunlight so that the sun's rays focus on the sausage.

INFERENCE

What outcome can be inferred from placing the barbecue in the sun so the rays focus on the sausage?

Using a COMPASS

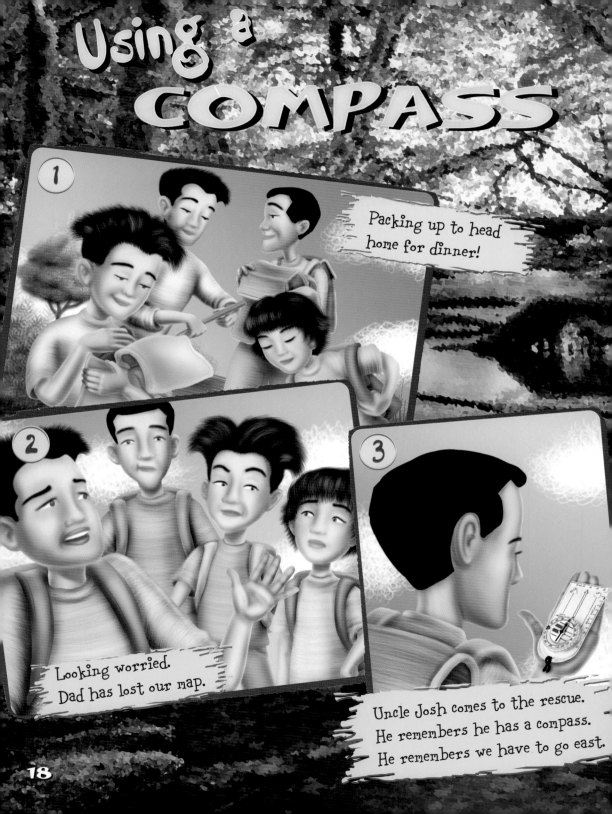

1. Packing up to head home for dinner!

2. Looking worried. Dad has lost our map.

3. Uncle Josh comes to the rescue. He remembers he has a compass. He remembers we have to go east.

USING A COMPASS

STEP ONE

To go east, find east on the compass housing, and turn the compass housing to face the direction of travel arrow.

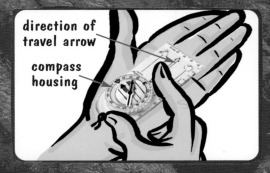

direction of travel arrow

compass housing

STEP TWO

Hold the compass flat in the palm of your hand and turn yourself, your hand and the compass until the red compass needle lines up with the orienting arrow.

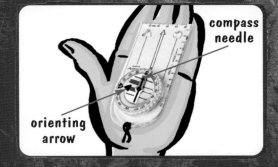

compass needle

orienting arrow

STEP THREE

Now you need to check that the red, or north part, of the compass needle points at north. This way you know you're going in the right direction!

COMPARE AND CONTRAST

Compare and contrast the types of Procedural Text. Look back to find examples of *How to Make*, *How to Find*, *How to Use*, *How to Do* texts.

Think About the Text

Making connections:
What connections can you
make with the text?

Experiencing irritation

Dealing with
frustration

Thinking about
sequence

Being
orderly

Text
to
Self

Thinking
logically

Being creative

Being patient

Having trust

Gaining a sense
of achievement

20

Text to Text

Talk about other stories you may have read that have similar features.
Compare the stories.

Text to World

Talk about situations in the world that might connect to elements in the story.

Planning a Procedural Text

THINK ABOUT...

Who will be reading the text.

THINK ABOUT...

The purpose of the text. Is it to:

SHOW HOW TO MAKE SOMETHING

SHOW HOW TO USE SOMETHING

SHOW HOW TO FIND SOMETHING

SHOW HOW TO DO SOMETHING

THINK ABOUT...

What information the reader will need to carry out the procedure.

A sequence that will make sense — which should come first, next . . .

How to Make	Statement of Goal	Materials	Steps in Order	→
How to Find	Statement of Goal		Steps in Order	→
How to Use	Statement of Goal		Steps in Order	→
How to Do	Statement of Goal		Steps in Order	→

THINK ABOUT...

How you can make your procedural text clear and easy to follow.

Use headings and subheadings to organise the information

Use photographs, diagrams, maps, cross-sections . . .

Use lists

Use numbered steps, bullet points . . . .

Procedural texts usually have:

- opening goals or aims, for example,
  - How to . . .
  - Making a . . .
- action verbs, for example, walk, turn, push, cut, pull . . .
- clear, concise language that is easy to follow
- words that indicate sequence — next, after, then, before . . .
- present or future tense
- lists of materials or ingredients needed
- headings, diagrams, drawings, photographs, maps, labels, tables, illustrations, bullets, arrows, captions, numbers
- rules or guidelines